Lively Advertising Cuts
of the
Twenties and Thirties

1,102 Illustrations of Animals, Food and Dining, Children, etc.

EDITED BY

Leslie Cabarga & Marcie McKinnon

Dover Publications, Inc.
New York

Publisher's Note

THE LINE ART produced in such copious amounts for consumer advertisements by largely anonymous artists of the 1920s and 1930s can surprise us today by its quality and quantity. In the pages of *Good Housekeeping, Collier's, Fortune,* the *Ladies' Home Journal,* and the *Saturday Evening Post,* these ads, usually devoid of color, solicited custom with their lively, simplified, focused designs and their usually buoyant moods. Readers of these magazines would also encounter innumerable little images sprinkled onto the pages merely to please the eye, images that came from typographers' catalogues expanded to include nontype elements. One of the largest of these was the *Type Peps* catalogue from the mid-1930s, many of whose cuts can be found in this collection.

Two of Leslie Cabarga's earlier Dover volumes—*1,001 Adver-* *tising Cuts from the Twenties and Thirties* and *Advertising Spo*[t] *Illustrations of the Twenties and Thirties*—have drawn largely o[n] the same sources while emphasizing some different subjects. Her[e,] for the first time, for example, are substantial sections devoted t[o] animals and to homes and housework, and other broadly usefu[l] topics such as food and drink, children, and services have no[w] been provided with dozens of new images.

Flappers and matrons, young blades and tycoons, infants an[d] children in many moods and costumes; work and play, duty an[d] pleasure; drollery and arch whimsicality, earthiness and glamou[r] (can you spot Rudolph Valentino and Charlie Chaplin here?)— the designer or artist will find over a thousand little evocations o[f] two eventful decades, from which emerge a broad picture o[f] American life as it was and as it hoped to be.

Contents

Copyright © 1990 by Leslie Cabarga and Marcie McKinnon.
All rights reserved under Pan American and International Copyright Conventions.

Published in Canada by General Publishing Company, Ltd., 30 Lesmill Road, Don Mills, Toronto, Ontario.
Published in the United Kingdom by Constable and Company, Ltd.

Lively Advertising Cuts of the Twenties and Thirties: 1,102 Illustrations of Animals, Food and Dining, Children, etc. is a new work, first published by Dover Publications, Inc., in 1990.

DOVER *Pictorial Archive* SERIES

Manufactured in the United States of America
Dover Publications, Inc., 31 East 2nd Street, Mineola, N.Y. 11501

Library of Congress Cataloging-in-Publication Data

Lively advertising cuts of the twenties and thirties : 1,102 illustrations of animals, food and dining, children, etc. / edited by Leslie Cabarga & Marcie McKinnon.
    p.   cm. — (Dover pictorial archive series)
    ISBN 0-486-26418-1 (pbk.)
    1. Commercial art—United States—History—20th century—Themes, motives. I. Cabarga, Leslie, 1954–   II. McKinnon, Marcie.   III. Series.
NC998.5.A1L58   1990
745.4′4973′09042—dc20
                                              90-3663
                                                CIP

Pets

HORSES

POULTRY

DOLLARS IN HARES

Sport Bodies

GUARDING POSTURE

Sport Bodies

AMERICA'S FASTEST SELLER

CRACKERS

SPARKLERS

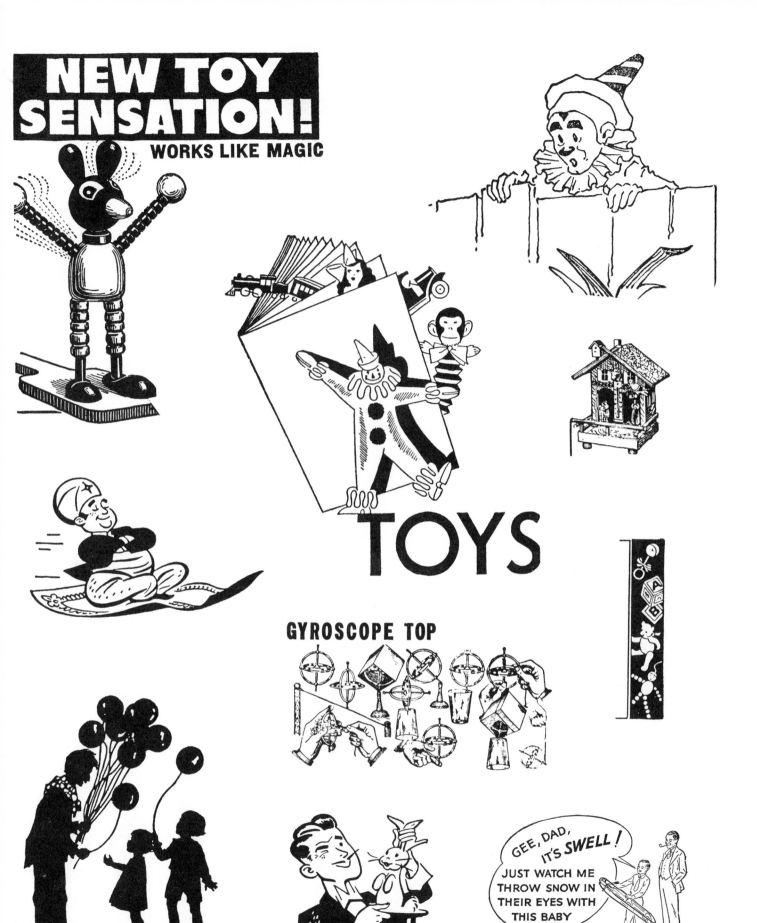

Card to Matchbox Trick

Mystify Your Friends With This Trick.

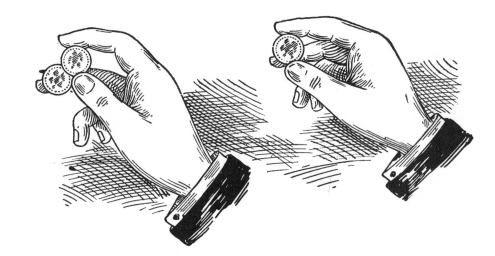

VENTRILOQUISM

Fortune Teller's Cards

Fig. 1

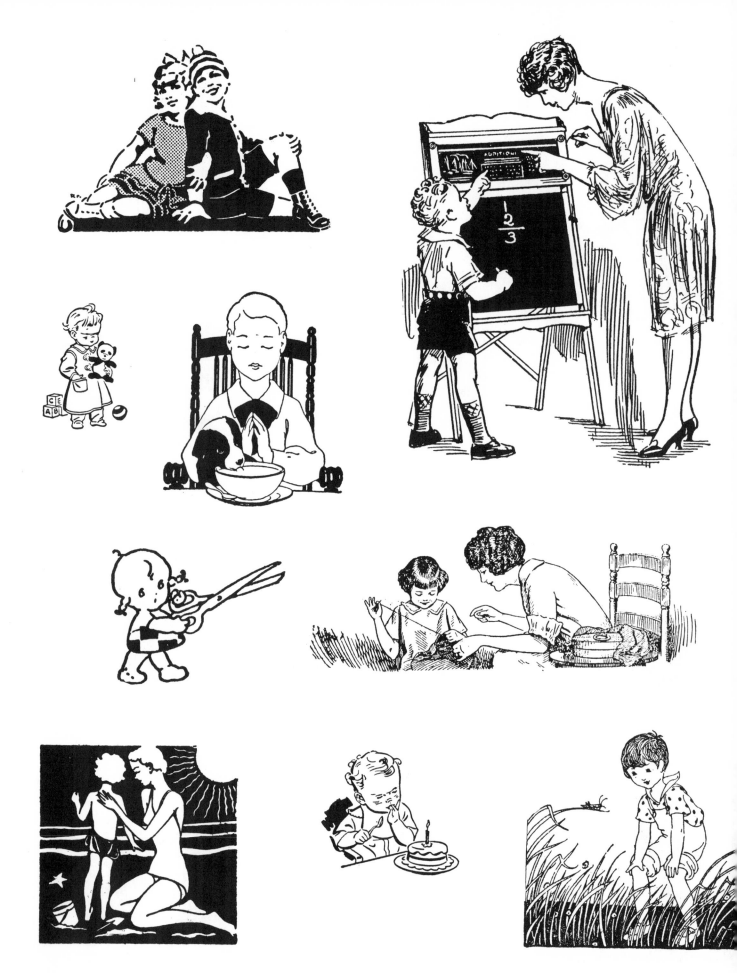

OPEN

ALL NIGHT

Frocks

Inside the comic illustration:

HEY... HOW
ABOUT
THAT BONE?

8 A. M.

8.15 A. M.

8.17 A. M.

HOME ❖ ECONOMICS

8.18 A. M.

Linens

Milady

To revive the
freshness
of your
dainty
garments

RADIATOR COVERS

Lingerie

Hosiery

Freed From Gray Hair

"What a funny idea!"

Jewelry

Beauty Shop

LINGERIE

Spring Fashions

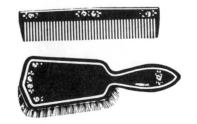

Pure Silk

AGE!

Dressmaker

A closet full of clothes — and nothing to wear!

The Shoe

**Men didn't
look twice at Mary**

Plenty for "Pretties"

Lingerie

PRETTY LADIES

Hosiery

Lingerie

Permanents

Lingerie

Hat Cleaners

Shoe Shining

Piano Tuning

All Laundry service

WASH

Better Vision

IXMC
WLMTIE
RSVTFMV

Hair Dressers

Fur Repairing

Optician

Laundry

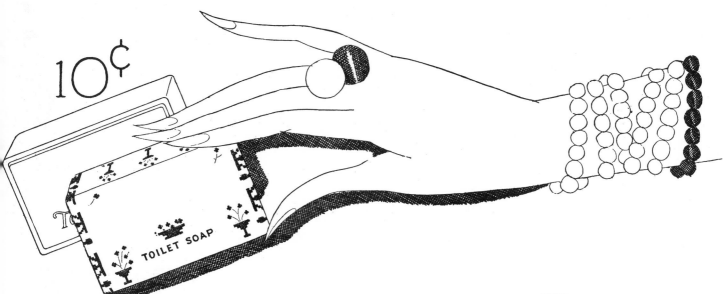

10¢

TOILET SOAP

We Shine

TYPEWRITER SERVICE RENT and REPAIR

FACIALS

Hair Cutting

CLEANERS

Ladies Hair Cutting

SHOE REPAIR

Ladies Hair Cutting

OPTICIAN

DRY CLEANING

LAUNDRY

Shoe Repair

Cleaners

We make Keys

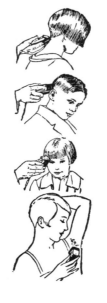

We call and deliver

Beauty Shop

Hair Bobbing

DELIVERY SERVICE

Cleaning and Pressing Service.

CLEANERS

Shoes Repaired

WHILE YOU WAIT

DRY CLEANERS

Cleaned

JUST LIKE NEW

MOVING? Call Us

TAILOR

Cleaning
Pressing
Repairing

SHOE SHINE

OPTICIAN

SHOE REPAIR

TRY OUR Pressing service

WE'LL BE ON TIME

LEAVING TOWN? Call us

TAXI phone us

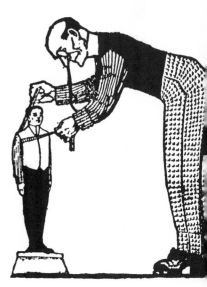

DRY CLEANERS

DRY CLEANERS

Up to the minute

HAIR CUTS

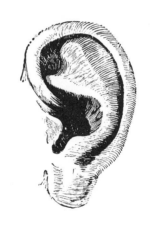

TOWEL SERVICE

Dress up

CLEANERS

PANTS MATCHED
TO ANY SUIT-

WHOOF
WOOF

MILK

OFFICE
UP→

FOR MEN ONLY

Haberdashery

BIG FREE OUTFIT

SET YOUR CLOCK AHEAD ONE HOUR TONIGHT

Did You Set Your Clock Ahead ?

20 YEARS FROM NOW?

40 YEARS FROM NOW?

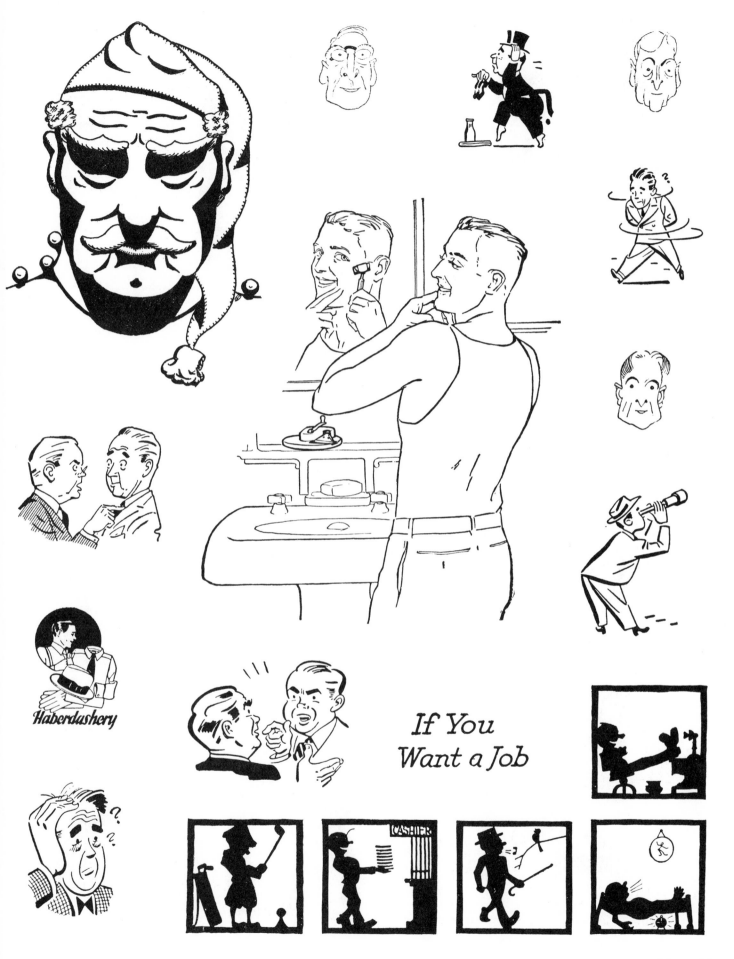

Haberdashery

If You Want a Job

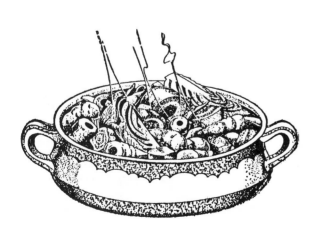

MEATS

Choice meats

Chicken Dinner's

CHOICE MEATS

Lunch

Try **OUR COFFEE** It's **DELICIOUS**

COFFEE AND NONE BETTER

ALWAYS GOOD COFFEE

Coffee and none better

Bakery

We have fine **Baked goods** YES SIR

Fine Food

Menu

Excellent Food

Dine & Dance

Menu

Service
our first thought

CHINA

soda
Fountain

Soda
Fountain

FOUNTAIN SERVICE

Food facts for Home Folks

A Department Devoted to feeding the family

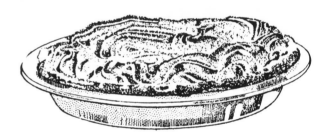

Milk Cream

The **IDEAL FOOD**

VITAMINS *for* **Growth** *and* **Health**

PROTEINS (Casein and Albumen) *for* **Muscle and Tissue Growth**

FAT (Cream) *for* **Fuel**

SUGAR (Lactose) *for* **Energy**

MILK

MINERALS *for* **Bone Growth**

FLUID *for* **Carrying off Wastes**

DAIRY

PureMilk

GROCERIES

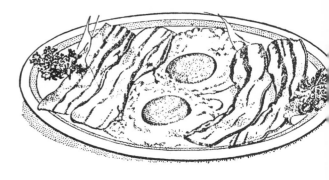

What to Eat
Easy lessons in nutrition

MEATS

DELICATESSEN

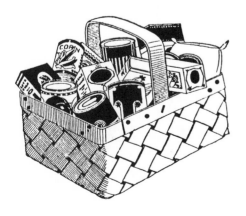

FISH MARKET

Delicious Sandwiches

When the Landscape looks like this

COCKTAIL LOUNGE and RESTAURANT

HOME COOKING

That will Please you

BEER
Lunches
Dinners
Suppers

DINE & DANCE

COCKTAIL LOUNGE

THERE'S A TAVERN IN THE TOWN WHERE GOOD FELLOWS Gather' Round

Beer Garden

BEER

wines

TAVERN

FOUNTAIN

SERVICE

CALL US FOR

Liquor

WE DELIVER

Liquor Store
all the better brands

Liquors and Wines

Liquors and Wines

California Wines
MADE FROM CALIFORNIA FRUITS

GOOD BEER · GOOD MUSIC

DINE and DANCE

FUN GALORE!
The TOWN'S
GAY SPOT
HURRY BACK

Cocktails
SO REFRESHING

¼ ROD
SCREWEYES

Peel glazed cloth
off face of patch

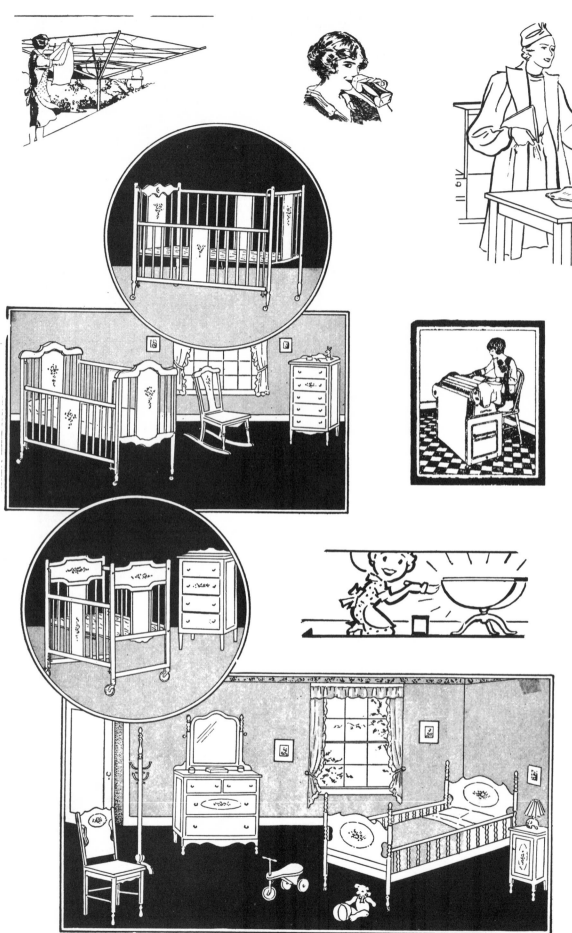

The
DRESS SIZE
ADJUSTMENT

The
UNDER-ARM
SHIELDS

The
ADJUSTABLE
HEM

The
MENDERS

WEDDING CAKES

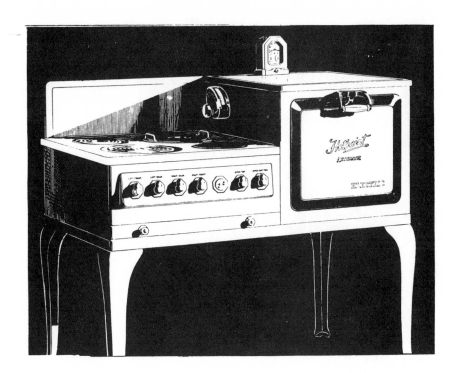

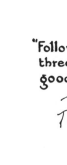

"Follow a thread of the goods"

DEEP FAT FRYING

JACK FROST

KITCHEN

SPARE Room

LAUNDRY

BATH Room

Only ⓵¢
a meal per person
to cook *electrically*

LINOLEUMS

MATTRESSES

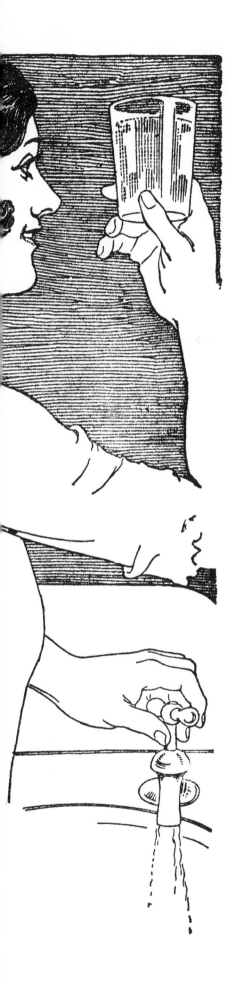

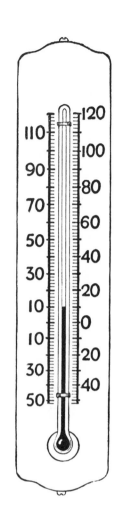

Home Decoration

Home Decoration

JAN. 1 New Resolutions 1929

FASTEST IN THE WORLD

A touch of the toe empties the tank.

SHADES

Get his
Christmas
Cigars
Here

CIGAR

3 for 50¢
15¢

2 for 25¢
10¢

CIGARS

POOL

Cigars and Tobacco